β

Books by Ross R. Olney

Farm Giants

Construction Giants

Ocean-going Giants

Imaging: Think Your Way to Success in Sports and
   Clasroom

IMAGING

Think Your Way to Success in Sports and Classroom

IMAGING:

*Think Your Way
to Success in Sports
and Classroom*

by ROSS R. OLNEY
and PATRICIA J. OLNEY

ATHENEUM · 1985 · NEW YORK

Library of Congress Cataloging in Publication Data

Olney, Ross Robert
  Imaging: think your way to success in sports and classroom.

Includes Bibliography
  SUMMARY: Explains techniques for developing a positive
attitude and for visualizing success in such phases of
life as sports, the classroom, public speaking, weight
control, and social situations.
1. Sports—Psychological aspects—Juvenile literature.
2. Learning, Psychology of—Juvenile literature.
3. Achievement motivation in children—Juvenile literature.
4. Imagination in children—Juvenile literature.
5. Visualization—Juvenile literature. [1. Visualization
2. Imagination. 3. Success. 4. Sports—Psychological
aspects. 5. Learning—Psychology] I. Olney,
Patricia J. II. Title.
GV706.4.04   1985   796'.01   85-7472
ISBN 0-689-31121-4

Contents

1   *Your Mind Will Help You Do Anything*   3

2   *Sure, But It Might Have Been Luck*   8

3   *There's Nothing Wrong With Daydreaming*   15

4   *Let's Get Scientific for Just a Moment*   21

5   *Be the Most Confident Person in Town*   27

6   *The Amazing "Confidence Tape"*   35

7   *Don't Let Them Get You Up-Tight*   39

 8   *Here's What Really Happens Inside*   43

 9   *You Can Be a Sports Hero*   51

10   *Exercise Your Brain as Well as Your Body*   56

11   *Attack Your Weaknesses, and Know Why*   59

12   *The Inner Peace Technique*   65

13   *You Must Learn to Concentrate*   71

14   *Using Imagery in Your Daily Life*   76

15   *One of the Worst Fears of All*   85

Index   92

IMAGING

*Think Your Way
to Success in Sports
and Classroom*

1

Your Mind Will Help You Do Anything

Professor Harold Hill was a con man, there was no doubt about that.

Oh, he was lovable, but in his own time he was still a crook. Hill was the main character in composer Meredith Willson's popular Broadway show, *The Music Man*. The show became a hit motion picture and Hill became famous around the world.

The "Professor's" scam was selling musical instruments to turn-of-the-century Midwestern parents with the promise of creating a town boys' band. The problem was that Hill had no musical training at all. There was no way he could teach the youngsters to play.

That didn't bother Hill, because by the time the final payments were received, he was, at the "last wave of the brakeman's hand on the last freight train out of town," gone. Hill's business became so successful in town after town that he added band uniforms to his line, increasing his profit substantially.

But how did he con the parents during the period of waiting for the instruments and then the uniforms? He used the famous Professor Harold Hill "Think System" for teaching. It was simple. You merely *thought* about playing the trumpet or clarinet or tuba. Hill wouldn't even allow his young students to blow into their horns. They were permitted to sit as a group and think about the Minuet in G. Nothing more. Sometimes they would hum together, holding their instruments in position.

A scam? A con? A rip-off? Even Hill, himself, admitted that it was.

But was it?

Today, Professor Harold Hill would be taken very seriously. Today we know that the simple con of Harold Hill could work. If he had believed in what he was doing, and convinced his young students to believe, the whole thing might have been possible.

In fairness to playwright Meredith Willson, the play ends with the young, rag-tag band actually rendering an almost recognizable Minuet in G before the townsfolk. Even the young bandsmen didn't understand why they were succeeding (nor did an astounded Professor Hill), but they were. A wonderful story.

And proof that what is well accepted now, the

process of thinking one's way to success in life, has been around for a long time.

Do you know what some athletes, especially Russian athletes, do for a big part of their workouts? They sit in the stadium and think about the whole thing. They visualize themselves winning the race, or throwing the javelin a greater distance, or jumping the highest bar. Some of them spend more time thinking about the event than they do practicing it. Because they believe it will work, it works.

American Olympic ice dancer Michael Seibert and his partner, Judy Blumberg, "practice in their minds."

"It sounds crazy," she says, "but it works."

A Simple Test

Try this simple experiment. Don't read ahead. Just do it step by step.

> Step 1 • Find a tree more than a few inches in dia-meter. Then collect a handful of small stones. Stand back ten or fifteen feet, then toss one half of the stones, one by one, at the three trunk. If you are an average stone-tosser, you will miss the tree more times than you hit it. Hitting a small tree trunk with pebbles isn't that easy.

> Step 2 • Here comes the fun (and relaxing) part of this experiment. You still have half of the stones. Sit back and take it easy for a few minutes. Think about the stones hitting the tree trunk. Visualize in your mind every single stone hitting the tree. Imagine that not one stone is going to miss.

Step 3 • Now concentrate even more. Try your best to imagine the tree trunk actually moving forward to where it is so near you couldn't possibly miss. Imagine it moving from side to side so that it is jumping in front of the stones you are tossing. Imagine the tree trunk wanting to get hit by the stones.

Step 4 • Now, one by one, throw the rest of the stones. Keep picturing in your mind that each toss is going to be perfect. As you toss each stone, visualize the tree jumping forward to meet it. Try to believe that you couldn't miss the tree if you wanted to. Try very hard to believe that you are going to hit the tree without trouble or effort.

Step 5 • This is IMAGERY. Some experts call it "guided" imagery, or visualization. This time you will hit the tree more often. If you don't, perhaps a bit more effort and concentration is necessary.

Science? Yes, imagery is a science. A brand new one. More and more, experts realize that imagery works, more and more athletes and scholars are using it to improve their performances. We all use it, in fact. The trouble is, most of us use it negatively. There will be no more of that!

Will It Work For You In a Positive Way?

The younger you are the better it will work. A younger mind is more flexible, more ready to accept new ideas. If you give it a chance, you can take control of your own life.

Consider the young basketball player who seemed to have a fine future in the game, but who was terrible at the foul line. He couldn't seem to hit the basket from the free throw line, but otherwise he was a fine player. His lack of skill at the foul line was hurting his game.

So he practiced long hours. The harder he worked, the worse he became. Maybe it was the pressure from his coach, or the pressure he was putting on himself with after-hours practice, but he wasn't improving at all.

So his coach decided to try imagery.

"Quit practicing free throws," he ordered. "Don't stand out there at the foul line beating yourself."

"Then what should I do, coach?" the desperate young player asked.

"Try this. Every time you see me on campus, visualize a perfect foul shot. Picture it in your mind every single time we meet, on the court, in the classroom, everywhere," said the coach. "See the ball go up and see it swishing through the net. See it over and over again. See yourself throwing perfect foul shots."

Almost immediately, the player's performance at the foul line dramatically improved.

Try it if you doubt. The same can work for you in any phase of your life.

2

Sure, But It Might Have Been Luck

Luck?

No. Not in the sense that it was some outside force, or fate, or some other factor that brought about the change. It wasn't luck if you consider luck to be something over which you have no control.

"With my luck, I'll probably crash . . . or trip . . . or get pneumonia . . . or fail." Don't you believe it, because if you do, it might well happen, and that is the only place where "luck" comes into the picture. Luck, according to most dictionaries, is the force that seems to operate for good or ill in a person's life. Luck is something that shapes opportunities, circumstances or events, but something we cannot really change.

Bill, a high school student, was worried about an upcoming history test. He was prepared, but he had psyched himself into believing that he was going to flunk. He had had a string of "bad luck." His car's fender had been creased, his wristwatch lost, and his dog had disappeared. Not only that, but he'd had a real fight with his girlfriend. It had not been Bill's week, and now he had an important history test to face.

He was sure he was going to fail it.

And he did. But it wasn't luck. It was believing he was going to fail. The fact was, the fender had been creased by a careless student who, when he realized what had happened, offered to pay. His wristwatch was located in the floor of his locker where it had fallen and his dog came home in a couple of days. The fight with his girlfriend was soon over.

But Bill, though he was prepared, still flunked the test—because he thought he would.

Reverse Imagery

If there is "reverse" imagery, it worked on Bill. Don't believe that you can't control luck, and don't believe anything but that you are going to succeed in what you are attempting. See yourself winning, or passing, or getting what you want. See it over and over again. If a negative thought creeps in (as it is almost sure to do at first) push it out and fill the space with belief. You will win more and more, and lose less and less.

Daydreaming

Is that all it is? Are you just supposed to sit around daydreaming about something rather than going out and doing it?

Ask yourself this question: Is daydreaming just a method of mental dawdling, a substitute for working at something?

If you answered yes, please reconsider. First of all, everybody daydreams. In fact, according to a study at Pennsylvania State University, people with high I.Q.'s appear to daydream more frequently and are more accepting of daydreaming. The study also indicated that people with lower I.Q.'s tend to feel guilty about daydreaming and even have negative thoughts about the content of their daydreams.

People with higher I.Q.'s also tend to enjoy their daydreams more. They are often refreshed and renewed after a daydream, stimulated to go on and to make constructive use of them.

Daydreams are imagery when used in this manner. If you daydream about something you hope to accomplish, or about an area in which you hope to improve, and you see these things in a positive manner, you are using imagery.

Aubrey is his school's top cross-country runner. At meets, Aubrey is generally considered the favorite in this sport that demands endurance and heart. Even when you are ready to drop, you must run on.

You wouldn't imagine that "daydreaming" would have any place in a rugged cross-country race, would you?

Aubrey just smiles, for he has a secret. He is a closet

daydreamer. He learned the technique from a book by Coach Mike Spino, resident running director at the Sea Pines Resort in South Carolina and director of the Esalen Sports Center. Spino suggests that imagery can be a great help to runners and gives specific advice. Aubrey took the advice to heart.

"When I'm tired . . . I mean, *really* tired . . . I visualize a giant hand helping to support me," Aubrey explains. "It works. It keeps me from falling. And when I'm sure I don't have one more stride and the finish line is still far away, I imagine a sky hook helping me along, tugging at me to keep me going. Then, when I can see the line in the distance, I visualize a tight wire between me and the finish. It gently pulls me along. I can feel it pulling.

"Yes, it works and it helps."

Coach Spino agrees. "Visualization techniques will be among the most important aspects of athletic training in the future," he says.

✓ How To Think Visually

The trick is to learn to think visually, to learn how to create in your mind a solid and realistic image or situation. Once you can do this, you will be on your way to using these images to improve your own performance in the classroom, in the school play, in the orchestra pit, on the athletic field, or wherever else you want to improve.

You can't do that, you say? You have difficulty creating a mental image. No problem. You can learn to do it with some simple exercises. Exercises will help you strengthen and stimulate your visual memory. This first one will be easy to do, but as in all things, practice will make it even more perfect.

The Reason for This Exercise

To help you practice creating solid visual images of a situation or activity.

The Supplies You Will Need

None

How To Do The Exercise

• Relax. Close your eyes. Visualize a scene from your past that is quiet and peaceful. Perhaps a lake you visited, a camp you once attended or any other peaceful spot. Do this for thirty seconds.

• Relax. Close your eyes. Visualize your most recent date or a friend. See the clothing he or she was wearing. Try to include some of the details such as color, accessories, even shoes. Do this for thirty seconds.

• Relax. Close your eyes. Visualize your school campus, or the sports field, or even a favorite food. Add details as they come to your mind, including colors, smells, or sounds. Do this for thirty seconds.

The Result You May Expect

Exercises such as these may be done anywhere, anytime, several times each day, to help you stimulate your visual memory. As the pictures come more easily to your mind, begin to add more and more details until you can see them almost as in life.

The idea is to be able to call such scenes to mind quickly and in detail, then study them over just as though you were there. Remember such things as the smells, the sounds, and the colors. If you are having a problem with them, don't even try until you are in a calm, undisturbed situation yourself. Sounds and other disturbances will make the exercises more difficult.

Let's Try Another Exercise

You can do this one along with the first one, or practice the first one until you feel you have acquired the skill of visualization of random things.

The Reason for This Exercise
To help you acquire the skill of visualizing a top performance of your own.

The Supplies You Will Need
None

How To Do The Exercise
• Choose a situation in which you would be involved. This can be in the classroom, on the sports field, or any other competitive activity. Now visualize yourself doing better than anybody else, winning the game, getting an A for your excellent paper, or scoring a difficult point. Do this for thirty seconds.

• Choose another situation and visualize it in the same way. Add details as they come to you. Do this for thirty seconds.

- One more time, pick a situation and visualize it. See yourself winning, even if you have never won before. Add details until you see it very clearly. Do this for thirty seconds.

The Result You May Expect

Now you are stimulating your visual memory in specific situations that might be competitive, where you might be a winner or a loser.

In both of the above exercises, the eyes should be closed. At least at first. Then, as you gain control of your visual memory, try them with your eyes open.

Here's a hint. When we are trying to visualize something that has happened in the past, the eyes generally tend to go up and to the left. When we are trying to visualize something that might happen in the future, the eyes tend to go up and to the right. So help yourself by doing it that way. If you are visualizing something from the past, look up and to the left. In the future, up and to the right.

Remember, these and any other exercises in this book can (and probably *should*) be done in time that is not being used for something else. Use time that might otherwise be wasted . . . standing in line, waiting at a bus stop, between classes, or while doing a normally boring task that is usually done by rote.

3

There's Nothing Wrong With Daydreaming

The trouble with Martha J. was that she wanted to be on the high school football team. This was a team of two-hundred-pound backs and two-hundred-fifty-pound linemen. Martha was a slip of a girl who weighed in wet at eighty-nine pounds. Nor was Martha all that sure how hard she wanted to work at get on the team. She was hoping they would just make a place for her in the backfield, perhaps as a quarterback, or maybe a running back . . . she wasn't sure.

All she knew was that she wanted to be on the team. She was quite good on the flag team and sure to become one of the cheerleaders next year, but she wanted to be a football player.

Can Martha get on the team through imagery? Possibly, but probably not. It is true that a person can do almost anything if they really want it and really set their mind to it. But most people, like Martha, don't *really* want something hard enough to sacrifice *everything* for it. So imagery probably won't work for Martha when it comes to getting on the team.

Martha is a daydreamer who dreams about exotic things she thinks will be exciting, but that she doesn't really want all that much.

Daydreaming can be good for us. "Imagining things," says one expert, "permits a trial-and-error approach without assessing any penalty for error."

Cindy was a girl who always thought things out. And with good results. If she was going to approach a teacher about a problem, she would first consider all the possible angles in her mind. She would see herself walking up to the teacher and hear what she was saying.

She would hear her teacher's reaction to that approach. Then she would try again in her mind, with a different approach, seeing each one as it happened. By the time Cindy actually approached the teacher with the problem, she had her methods well tested and generally knew what the result would be.

✓Daydreaming Is Visualization

Experiments have shown that the body actually begins to contract its muscles as you daydream about an activity. You may be relaxing . . . you *should* be relaxing at first . . . but still your muscles begin to condition themselves to the activity you are seeing in your mind.

Many scientists believe that in only a few more decades humans will begin to learn to control the things around them by brain power. They might be able to move things about by thinking about moving them. This is all in the future, but we are at the beginnings of this today. And you can *use* it. You can use the power of your mind and make your body respond.

Meanwhile, the United States Olympic ski team used the services of psychologist Richard Suinn, who is with the Department of Psychology at Colorado State University. Dr. Suinn is an expert in the use of fantasy in athletics. The skiers were trained to imagine themselves making their ski runs over and over again. They would visualize the slopes in their minds as they thought out every problem, every bump and every slick spot. Such mental rehearsals had a positive effect on subsequent runs down the slopes.

Medicine

Even more startling, more and more doctors are recognizing that the best approach to healing . . . perhaps the only approach . . . must involve the body *and the mind*. Disharmony between the two can result in the very illness you might fear most, while harmony can not only speed healing but help to maintain good health.

If you think yourself healthy, you will be more healthy. If you think you are going to get well, you will get well much faster.

You can hurt yourself in the same way. Worry may be one of the greatest health threats of all. A study in the *New England Journal of Medicine* shows the great influence that mental health may have on physical health. The study involved 188 Harvard graduates over a period of thirty years.

Mental health was measured in terms of job satisfaction, happiness in marriage, use of tranquilizers and visits to psychiatrists. Those who seemed the most psychologically fit seemed to be the most physically fit. Those suffering from chronic anxiety, depression or emotional maladjustment seemed more likely to develop heart disease, cancer, diabetes, cirrhosis, emphysema and other maladies. Although not proof positive (since emotional distress often precedes physical illness) the conneciton is there. Positive thinking can effect positive cures.

Author Norman Cousins was diagnosed to have ankylosing spondylitis, a degenerative disease of the connective tissue. He was critically ill. At best, he could only hope for eventual paralysis. Already he was in deep pain and his hands were becoming useless.

"The prognosis," said Cousins, "was progressive paralysis; I was told I'd have to make a choice between having my body freeze sitting up or lying down." His chances for recovery were listed at one in five hundred by doctors.

"No!" said Cousins, a positive man. Since help from others was no longer available, since the doctors had given up, he took on his own treatment. "You tend to your business," he told the doctors, "and I'll tend to mine."

With the earlier work of Dr. Hans Selye in mind, Cousins checked out of the hospital. Selye's work indicated that stress could adversely affect body chemicals and cause illness. "Besides," said Cousins, a hospital is "the last place someone sick should go." Cousins checked into a comfortable hotel.

He borrowed a movie projector and some classic reels of *Candid Camera* from his friend, Alan Funt. He also obtained some Marx Brothers films, E.B. and Katharine White's *Subtreasury of American Humor*, Max Eastman's *The Enjoyment of Laughter*, and the numerous works of P.G. Wodehouse, James Thurber, Ogden Nash, S.J. Perelman and Bennett Cerf.

"I made an interesting discovery," he said. "Ten minutes of solid belly laughter would give me two hours of pain-free sleep." What he had discovered was catalogued by doctors ten years later: Laughter . . . and a generally happy, relaxed state . . . produces proteins called endorphins. These are natural morphinelike painkillers.

"At the end of the critical two weeks, during which I took the love, laughter and ascorbic-acid (vitamin C) therapy," said Cousins, "I was able to move my thumbs . . . and I knew I was going to make it all the way." Eventually, he was able to play tennis three times each week.

Psychologist Adelaide Bry reveals how you can channel your mental powers to help prevent or cure disease and take control of your life in her book *Visualization: Directing the Movies of Your Mind.*

Dr. Bry cites the work of Harold Burr, an anatomist from Yale Medical School, who showed that all the protein in the body is renewed at least every six months. Thus, technically speaking, not one particle of ourselves is identical to what it was only six months ago.

It follows, according to Dr. Bry, that the power of the mind can create and recreate the body and its cells. It is possible that by concentrating our mental powers, we could destroy tumors, make cells whole again, change the pressures in our body, raise or lower our temperatures, protect ourselves from toxins, shift pain about or eliminate it, and help medicines to help our body. Any part of us that we can imagine in our brain can be strengthened or weakened.

How can this be? How can the power of the mind control the actions of the body? There are many areas where the body and mind work precisely together. Clinical psychologist Joseph E. Shorr agrees in his book, *Go See the Movie in Your Head.*

You've seen it plenty of times. Andrea blushes when she gets embarrassed. Her mind causes her skin to flush because of something it perceives. David yawns because his mind tells him he is bored. June's heart speeds up when she is frightened.

Visualization is known to have a definite effect on the body's electrical field. If you simply *imagine* yourself running, according to psychologist Edmund Jacobson, the muscles involved with jogging actually contract a small but measurable amount.

4

Let's Get Scientific for Just a Moment

There are pathways between that part of the brain where pictures are stored and the involuntary nervous system that controls such functions as sweating, blood pressure and digestion.

When she is mentally stressed about something, Judy feels her stomach becoming upset. If she eats something under these conditions, something she normally enjoys, she becomes ill.

In Judy, and in all of us, these pathways between the brain and the nervous system link the pituitary gland with the adrenal cortex. Thus a picture in our mind has an impact on every cell in our bodies.

Through mental images we can do more than simply think and analyze what happens to us. We can experience and control it directly. You can bring about a solution that seems impossible by tuning into your mental images, *if you believe it.*

Practice . . . Practice . . . Practice

Remember the Russian athletes who *think* about working out rather than really working up a sweat practicing? Dr. Charles Garfield reported that some of Russia's top athletes spend up to seventy-five percent of their training time on mental preparation.

"You see stories about a one-hundred-and-twelve-pound grandmother lifting a Buick to save her grandchild," he said. "The Soviets have been looking at this psychological-physiological connection for over thirty years. They wanted to know whether it could be harnessed and whether athletes could use it in competition. Both answers are yes."

Russian athletes at first attain a state of deep relaxation. They visit the scene of their event in their minds and set a maximum performance level for themselves. Then they visualize "as clear as a color TV picture" the successful completion of the contest, with them winning.

More often than not, they win.

"Wart Healers" and "Spoon Benders"

Many years ago, parents took a child with warts to some old man or woman known as a "wart healer." The healer would go through an impressive routine and tell the child that because of this all of the child's warts would go away. Often enough the warts would soon fade.

Because of the performance of the healer? No, almost certainly it was because of the faith of the child. Because of the power of the mind of the child to believe so strongly that the "cure" would work, it worked. The child believed it would happen and the subconscious produced the desired result.

How about spoon bending? In 1972, Israeli psychokinesist Uri Geller appeared on a BBC television show for children and suggested that his young viewers try to bend spoons and forks themselves, as Geller said he had been doing, by the power of the mind. Several youngsters were said to be successful, according to published reports.

Do you believe it? You can try it, or you can take the word of physicist Peter R. Phillips, a professor at Washington University with an undergraduate degree from Cambridge University in England and a doctorate from Standard University in California. With a grant of $500,000 from the McDonnell Foundation, Phillips has set up the McDonnell Laboratory for Psychic Research to study things like spoon bending.

If you are going to test the power of your own mind, "Don't pick one of your best spoons," warns Phillips. Many such experts believe there are any number of children who can bend a spoon by the power of their mind.

How To Use Your Daydreams

There are nine ways you can use your daydreams to make them work for you. Even in a society like ours that has always put a premium on *doing* instead of *dreaming*, recent psychological studies have shown that daydreaming, also called "creative imagining," is a key factor in mental health. Daydreaming can also be one of our most constructive mental activities.

It is said that Michelangelo once looked at a block of marble that had been spoiled by the cutters at the quarry, but he saw in his mind its potential for beauty. So he carved his famous statue of David.

Surveys show that today more than nine out of every ten of us engage in some form of daydream almost every day. Psychologist Morton Wagman says that males tend to imagine themselves as heroes of some adventurous or dramatic situation while females have more gentle daydreams about their school, their work, their famiiles or their homes.

Here is how to use your daydreams.

• Use them to help solve intellectual problems. When the brain is in an "alpha" state, such as when you are daydreaming, it is more likely to be receptive to flashes of insight. Daydreams can bring back long-forgotten bits of knowledge that can provide answers to perplexing problems.

• "I use daydreams to help prepare for difficult situations," said one student. "Once I had to give up a dog I loved. I found myself visualizing the scene where I left him at his home. It was heartbreaking, but the dreams helped me work up to the time when I actually did give him away because they always included a happy home for him and eventual acceptance by me."

✓ • Daydreaming can be used to help you test future plans or choices by giving you the chance to see how each choice might work out. In your mind's eye you can make physical changes or engage in important discussions, then pick the ones that worked out the best. You can make mistakes without paying a price.

• Use your daydreams to work out frustrations. Student Betty works in the school office and is often frustrated by adult employees who treat her like a child. "I just go back over some of the conversations we've had that drove me up a wall, but this time I make them come out the way *I* want them to. This mental 'blowing off steam' really helps."

• John uses his daydreams to fulfill an ambition that is at the moment out of reach. "I want this new car, but there is no way I can afford it on my income as a part-time fast food restaurant employee. So I just dream about the new car for now. I've gotten in and driven it away a hundred times. It's *beautiful*. Someday, I'll be able to buy it."

• Use your daydreams just as famous athletes do. Practice a skill or a presentation over and over again in your mind. Mental practice gives you a chance to look over your performance and change it if you wish. Meanwhile, it is certain to improve your "live" performance when that time comes.

• Use daydreams to solve problems, but not in the "direct" way. You may worry over a solution for hours, but nothing happens. So set aside the problem and "drift" awhile. "All the information is still in your mind," says one student who uses this approach, "but you're giving your mind a chance to see it from a different point of view. Your mind has a chance to fit together the ideas in a different way, and that can lead to new insights and solutions."

• With daydreaming you can tap buried resources of strength to be used in difficult projects. "When I get nervous about making a speech," says one student, "I recall how I overcame the problem in past speeches. I did it then, I say to myself, and I can do it now."

• Improve your health with daydreaming. At the first sign of a headache, for example, relax and imagine yourself in a situation where your hands are being warmed and your head is being cooled. Lying on a beach under an umbrella might work for you. Listen to the waves on the beach. Even migraine sufferers can in this way increase the blood flow to their hands and decrease the flow to their heads, stopping the painful dilation of blood vessels that cause headaches.

Hospital studies indicate that a patient who can envision what will happen during and after surgery, how much pain can be expected, will have less pain and will make a faster recovery.

Daydreaming, according to psychologist Robert Goldenson, "renews our vitality and 'restoreth the soul'. Call it daydreaming, building castles in the air, starry-eyed fantasy or just plain unwinding, every child and every adult needs this kind of escape."

5

Be the Most Confident Person in Town

Alexandra Reinhardt, LPGA professional golfer, once explained the difference between herself and Nancy Lopez. "She'll stand over a ten-foot putt *knowing* it will drop. I'll stand over the same putt thinking that if I miss it will cost me five hundred dollars."

Confidence

You must believe you can pass the test, or win the game, or score the touchdown, or do well in the school play . . . or impress your date next time out. If you do not believe it, nobody else will, and you'll stand a greater chance to fail.

Speaking of confident golfers, in the second round of the 1984 PGA tournament, Lee Trevino hit a five iron on a par three hole. He hit it so well that, "I was posing for pictures" as the ball sailed toward the green, confessed Trevino.

✓ A Confidence Test

How ready are you to win, to achieve, to excel? The following quiz will rate you. If you rate well, go for it! If your score indicates a lack of confidence, look over the areas where you have rated yourself down. You'll see where you have to improve as you learn more and more about imagery.

Each question should be rated on a scale of truth from 1 to 4. If you *strongly agree* with the statement, write a number 1 on a piece of paper. If you *mildly agree*, write number 2. If you *mildly disagree* with the sttaement, write number 3. If you *strongly disagree* with the statement, write number 4. It's easy and it's fun, and nobody will see the answers but you . . . and you will be able to change them as you retake the test. Remember that these are your evaluations of yourself and not what others think of you. Don't go for the obvious answers, and the test will help you improve your confidence.

Then, after awhile, you can take the test again.

---

1. I am well above average at anything I try.
2. I know my areas of strength.
3. I know my areas of weakness.
4. I learn from my mistakes.
5. I am able to watch experts and learn from them.

6. My mental rehearsals always show me achieving.
7. I have specific goals.
8. I never say "I can't."
3. I enjoy trying something entirely new.
10. I believe a top performer is made, not born.
11. I would rather improve and lose than remain static.
12. If I wanted to climb a mountain, I'd learn how to do it.
13. I don't mind sharing my winning secrets.
14. I approach a task positively, not negatively.
15. I would rather play well and lose than play poorly and win.
16. I am not embarrassed when I lose if I have done my best.
17. I can learn from those with less skill.
18. I enjoy teaching others my skills.
19. I don't worry too much about what others think.
20. If I lose, I use the loss to improve.
21. I spend practice time on my weakness, not my strengths.
22. I rarely compare my own performance with others.
23. I know I can improve my performance or my grades.
24. I never use lack of practice as an excuse for losing.
25. I set and reset personal goals.
26. I don't believe in luck.
27. I enjoy learning new techniques.
28. I still spend considerable time practicing or studying.
29. I feel I am as tough as those I'm competing with.
30. I am not self-conscious if others are watching.

Add up the numbers you have circled. Your score will fall between 30 and 120. Here's how to rate yourself.

30–50 • You are a dynamo of self-confidence, perhaps too much so. Be careful that you are not merely over-confident.

51–65 • You are normally self-confident. Work to improve in any of the areas where you scored higher, but don't worry. You'll do fine.

66–90 • Give some serious thought to working on the areas where you scored highest. You're OK, but you can stand a shot of confidence.

Over 91 • You are probably more confident than you think. Be careful of too much modesty or people will walk over you. Work on all the high score areas.

You *should* have more confidence than anybody. You are at an age of achievement in academics and sports. Your mind is sharp and your body, though generally strong and healthy, will do what your mind tells it to do. Go for it!

When Olympic decathlon champion Bruce Jenner walked on the field in Montreal in 1976, he *knew* he was going to win. There was no doubt in his mind even before his series of events started. He did have a worry, but that was on the day or two before the Olympics.

"I might have caught a cold, or come down with the flu," he admits with a grin. "If I had, it would have affected my performance. But on that morning, when I walked onto the field feeling great, I knew I would *win*."

He did, with a new world record performance in the grueling series of events.

Such confidence, when correctly directed, is a wonderful force. Think back for a moment to the last time you saw a loser, or a losing team, or a student who does poorly in classroom work. As a general rule, these people come up to their own expectations.

Are you a hockey fan? Do you recall the Los Angeles Kings during the 1983–84 season? The team had one of the best scoring lines in all of hockey, the "Triple Crown Line" of Marcel Dionne, Charlie Simmer and Dave Taylor. Individually, these three players were top scorers, and working together they were dynamite. Dionne, himself, was one of the best players in the history of hockey. Several other players were outstanding. The team had plenty of talent.

Yet, when the Kings skated onto the ice, they appeared to be losers. They came out of the locker room grim, with their heads down and frowns on their faces. They were having no fun at all. Even loyal fans began to realize that the team was going to lose the game. From the looks of the team, they felt the same way.

So, even with rare flashes of brilliance, the team did lose most of their games. Occasionally they were "up," and when they were they managed to beat the top teams in the league. But more often they were down, lackluster, unsure of their own ability. Though full of talent, they had branded themselves as losers and they lost game after game.

With Dionne, Simmer, Taylor, and several other fine players, they didn't even make the playoffs in a sport where almost every team gets into the final run for the Stanley Cup.

Don't allow this to happen to you.

Coaches can hurt players, especially young players, by being negative. You've heard them. "Now don't strike out!" they might shout at a little leaguer stepping up to the plate. This can cause the young player to visualize striking out. Instead, the coach might consider saying "I know you are going to hit the ball hard!" If you think you are going to lose, you probably will. If you think you are going to win, you will act like a winner . . . and this will help you win (even to the extent of disturbing your opponent so that he will lose).

In his book *Feeling Good: The New Mood Therapy*, Dr. David D. Burns lists three principles.

1. All of our moods are created by our thoughts. "You feel the way you do right now," explains Dr. Burns, "because of the thoughts you have at the moment."
2. When you feel negative or depressed, it is because your thoughts are dominated by " pervasive negativity." The whole world looks dark and gloomy. What's worse, "you'll come to believe that things really are as bad as you imagined them to be."
3. Negative thoughts almost always contain gross distortions. "Twisted thinking is the exclusive cause of nearly all of your suffering," says Dr. Burns.

In Dr. Burns's technique of Cognitive Therapy, patients listen to their own negative thoughts. This trains the patient to recognize these "inner saboteurs" and silence them. Try it on yourself. Beware of the following self-defeating thought patterns.

• Black and white thinking, like the "straight A" student who gets one "B" and thinks she is a total failure. There are shades of gray, you know.

• Overgeneralization that says one bad experience means that you are going to have "bad luck" forever, or a "streak" of bad luck.

• Taking the worst part of one situation and stretching it to cover the entire matter.

• Automatic discounting, such as when somebody compliments you and you brush it aside with the feeling that you are "second rate" and didn't really deserve the compliment.

• Jumping to a bad conclusion, looking into the future and seeing only disaster.

• Magnification and minimization, when you see your faults much greater than they are and your good points much less.

• Emotional reasoning, where you feel guilty, thus you must *be* guilty. You must challenge this reasoning for proof.

• *Should* thoughts, when you say, "I should do this," will only make you feel more guilty, and will not motivate you to do something.

• Irrational labeling, where you say, "I am a failure," instead of, "I made a mistake."

• Too much personalization, where you say "whatever happens, it is my fault," instead of realizing that you are responsible for your actions as others are for theirs.

List your negative thoughts, read and study them, then substitute more objective thoughts to replace the ones that make you depressed or negative. Remember the advice of Dr. Burns. Your feelings are feelings and not necessarily facts. You *can* cope. Don't base your opinion of yourself on your achievements. Treat yourself as a beloved friend, as an esteemed visitor you would not insult or peck about weaknesses or imperfections. As you would do for a friend or visitor, make yourself comfortable and confident.

6

The Amazing "Confidence Tape"

Everybody can't have the pure confidence of Olympian Bruce Jenner, at least not at first. Everybody can't be so sure of themselves. We all have varying degrees of confidence in our own ability. Even though you have studied, or rehearsed, or practiced hard, you may at first still have that inner feeling that you are going to fail, or be upstaged, or beaten.

What the Los Angeles Kings needed, and what you might need, is the help of a "Confidence Tape."

Let's set up a situation, then you can adjust it to your own circumstance.

Bob is getting ready for a racquetball game with Kathy next week. Bob is fairly new at the game, Kathy is an expert. Bob wants to do well for more reasons than winning. He really hopes to impress Kathy and perhaps get to know her better.

He knows the game well enough. He understands all the racquetball tricks of guarding the center of the court and changing the pace of the game to upset his opponent's style. But Bob wants more. He wants to *win* the game. And if he should lose, he wants to lose with grace after giving it everything he has. There is, however, a problem.

Though he plays a reasonable game of racquetball, Bob feels deep down that there is a very good chance Kathy will humiliate him on the court. He needs a shot of confidence.

A shot of confidence is something he can get, and it isn't difficult. He has a tape recorder (a cassette recorder is perfect) and that is all he needs. Bob makes a tape of his own voice.

"I feel *great*. I know the game well and I have played it enough to be pretty good at it. I know how to play to my best advantage by slowing things down and not allowing my opponent to overwhelm me.

"I am walking onto the court and I am *ready*. I am calm and I feel sure I am going to play well. My racquet feels good in my hand and the court feels familiar. I am ready for this game. I have worked hard and practiced hard and I know the game of racquetball. I check over my equipment, then calmly and confidently put on my gloves and glasses.

"The heavier beating of my heart is not anxiety, but just my body getting ready for the game, my juices speeding up in anticipation of some fun, my muscles getting toned up to *win*."

Bob goes on with the tape of his own voice, describing his positive feelings and emotions, as the game progresses. He tells how he serves into the corner and how difficult it is far Kathy to return the serve. He describes some of his own great shots.

He tells himself how he is feeling. He is refreshed, stimulated, and not tired at all. He keeps track of the score on his tape. He describes the game as it progresses, stressing how well he is doing. Eventually the final shots are served, he returns them perfectly, and wins the game.

Bob's tape is ready. So he plays it back. It sounds fine. For the next week, Bob listens to the tape whenever he can. He turns it on and listens to it several times every night before he goes to bed. Since Bob's recorder has an automatic shut-off, he plays it as he is going to sleep every night. By the day of the game, Bob's confidence is much improved.

He is certain to do better in the game then he would otherwise have done.

You can do the same with any activity you are approaching. It doesn't have to be an athletic competition. Cynthia made a tape to help her prepare for an appearance in her class play. She knew her lines, but she was concerned that she wouldn't do well in the play. So her tape described exactly how she arrived at the theater, how well she felt, how sure she was that everything was going to be just fine. She even repeated some of the key lines of the play on the tape, lines from scenes that bothered her.

Later, everybody remarked about how calm and confident Cynthia was during the performance, and how well she did in the show.

A Confidence Tape will work in classroom situations, too. It will help you pass a test, or make a report, or deal with a teacher.

Try it. It'll work for you.

7

Don't Let Them Get You Up-Tight

Did you know that if you dream you are having a close call, you will often sweat and twitch and your heart will speed up. If your mind believes (because of the dream) that you are in trouble, your body will react to the trouble. Your mind controls your body. There was never any real danger, but your brain didn't know that. So it caused the physical reactions in your body in an effort to help you.

How Tense are You?

Here's a simple test to determine your level of tension, or stress. Just write one of the numbers, after each statement, on a piece of paper according to how you feel about yourself. If you *strongly agree* with the statement, write number *1*. If you only *mildly agree* with the statement, write number 2. If you *mildly disagree* with the statement, write number 3 and if you *strongly disagree* with the statement, write number 4.

---

1. On an important occasion, my hands feel cold and I tend to perspire.
2. I tend to hurry through important things, to get them over as quickly as possible.
3. I worry, really worry, about an upcoming test or competition.
4. I rarely or never try something new at a critical time even though it could be a better way of doing it.
5. If I find myself making a mistake, I tend to go ahead instead of stopping and starting over.
6. I tend to forget names, facts, or plays under pressure.
7. If I start out poorly, I tend to continue on the same way.
8. I believe very much in "Murphy's Law" (that if something *can* go wrong, it *will*).
9. I am very critical of myself.
10. When before a group, I feel I am the least one of all.
11. I find it very difficult to "small talk" with my peers or superiors.
12. I am afraid of the dark, or the different, or the unique.
13. I am usually worried about saying "the wrong thing."
14. I suffer from "stage fright."

15. I tend to be second to try something rather than first.
16. When the chips are down, I'm afraid I might fail so I tend to tighten up.
17. I prefer to do something alone rather than have somebody watch me doing it.
18. I would rather write something than speak it.
19. The more I try to concentrate, the more nervous I become.
20. I frequently have bad dreams.

Your score will fall between 20 and 80. Add up your scores then rate your "anxiety level" on the following scale.

20–30 • You are a real "nervous Nellie," but don't worry, there's hope.

31–45 • You are probably much cooler than you think, but you are still pretty anxious about things around you.

46–60 • You are average where anxiety is concerned. You can improve, but this isn't too bad. You'll be all right.

61–80 • Don't kid yourself. Almost *nobody* is *this* calm. But if you are, congratulations. You should have no trouble with imagery.

Not that some anxiety is going to ruin you. Anxiety can be useful and appropriate if it is controlled. More about this later.

Meanwhile, you've probably seen certain spoiled sports figures throw a "choke" sign at their opponent after a particularly bad play. They bring their hand up and clutch their throat in a derogatory gesture designed to cut further into the opponent's confidence during a low moment.

There is scientific backing for this, too. The body goes into a preparedness state in the face of any danger (losing, looking bad, fear, etc.). You've probably awakened yourself at night during a nightmare and found your heart beating hard and your skin sweaty. Or maybe you have had a near miss in your car and reacted by these physical signs of danger, even though the danger, in both cases, was never real or never really happened.

These methods of the body preparing itself for danger are automatic and are designed to help us when we need it. They are not helpful in cases where the "danger" is only anxiety over an upcoming performance in the classroom or on the athletic field.

8

Here's What Really Happens Inside

Let's say you are getting really tense about an upcoming situation. Whether or not there is *reason* for the tension, your body sends a signal to the hypothalamus, which releases a hormone that triggers the pituitary gland. This gland sends a hormone (ACTH), which orders the adrenal gland to release other hormones with names that might sound familiar to you . . . adrenaline, norepinephrine, and cortisone.

These hormones help to prepare your body and mind for the critical situation you have indicated by your tension. So your heartbeat speeds up and you begin to pant to give your body a chance to release carbon dioxide more quickly. Your muscles tighten, *all* of your

43

muscles and not just the ones you need for a legitimate task. Even the muscles around your lungs and throat begin to tighten and this results in shallowness and even shortness of breath. So you breathe even more rapidly.

It is possible that if the situation were severe enough, you would actually choke to death. All because of tension over an upcoming task.

That's why athletes indicate a "choke" to each other. They hope that anxiety or tension will cause an opponent to hurt his or her performance.

If you can be made to believe that you are actually choking up (by the gestures they might make to you), your performance could be substandard . . . and they will win. Don't allow anybody to cause you to use your mind, and the resulting reactions in your body, to help to defeat you. Ignore them and go about your own business, doing the best you can . . . as most professional athletes do.

Sometimes a·teacher will add to your tension by ominously suggesting, "OK, there is going to be a test tomorrow, and it is going to be a tough one." They might better say, "Hey, we're going to have a little test, but you are all sharp students and you should have no trouble with it. If you are at all concerned, do a little extra studying on pages so and so."

Hear it that way, no matter how the teacher says it, and you'll be a step ahead of everybody else.

Assess Your Own Level of Anxiety

Ask yourself the following questions. Write down your answers so that you can study them, and use them.

✓ 1. Were my thoughts positive or negative before the test?
✓ 2. Was I most worried about a particular area of the test?
3. When did I feel most anxious?
4. Was I sure I was going to fail?
5. Was I worried about what my friends and my parents might think?

You can become more and more aware of negative thoughts if you bring them out in the light and study them. Once they are exposed, you can begin to rehearse yourself away from them.

You Can Use Tension

All of these pent-up workings of your body can be turned to your advantage through imagery. You can use them to improve your performance. Remember what is happening. Your body is preparing to face an emergency. The trick is, don't allow these preparations to cause you to choke.

Meanwhile, you are being provided with extra chemicals for an extra effort. If you are confident that you are going to succeed, if you are seeing yourself hitting a home run, or passing the test with flying colors, or scoring the winning basket, or driving long and true off the tee, these chemicals can help you rather than hurt you.

Golfer Jack Nicklaus uses the extra adrenaline to hit longer drives. Of course, he is confident that he is going to hit well in the first place, so the preparation of his body only increases his drive. Another golfer might be sure that he is going to slice, or hook, so the extra adrenaline only causes him to slice or hook deeper into the rough.

In a sense, you are going to use your tension to help you relax and do a better job.

Did you ever watch champion high jumper Dwight Stones preparing for a jump? Stones actually talks to himself. He stares at the bar as he gets ready to start his run. Then he talks. You can see him carrying on a conversation with himself, complete with gestures and facial expressions. He is telling himself where the bar is and how he is going to clear it. He doesn't start his run until he has convinced himself that he is going to succeed.

Nicklaus also talks to himself. And he answers himself, too. In fact, he once four-putted a hole. "I apologized to myself as I walked off the green," he confessed. Then he continued with a grin. "The trouble was, I couldn't bring myself to accept my apology."

Does all of this mental preparation embarrass Stone or Nicklaus? Obviously not. They do it, and they are two of the greatest athletes in sports.

Why should they be embarrassed?

Stress and tension can hurt your performance if they are not used to help it.

A Classroom Test? Go For It!

First of all, stop worrying. No matter how well or how poorly prepared you are for the test, worry will only hurt your performance. Worrying about a test will probably lower the grade you would have received if you have gone ahead without worry, regardless of your preparation. Easy to say? Sure, but don't knock it until you have tried it. Attempt to keep your emotions out of the matter. You have studied well (or maybe not so well) and now the time has come to take the test.

Young lawyers taking the "bar" exam are a perfect example of students in a most stressful situation. They have studied for years for this one moment. They are going to take a series of comprehensive tests, the result of which will determine whether or not the years have been wasted. If they pass, they will be allowed to hang out a shingle and practice their new profession, and perhaps earn the living they have been striving for in school. If they fail, no matter how perfect their grades were in law school, they can do nothing but try again . . . and again. They *must* pass the bar, or they have failed.

Oh, there are other things a law school graduate can do, but until they pass they bar, they cannot practice law. They cannot take on clients and handle their cases in court. Worse, these students have had years to think about this exam. They have heard all the horror stories about failures and trick questions and varying grading practices. They are on the line.

Again and again, those students seem to do better who approach the bar exam calmly and with an attitude that they are going to do their best come what may. They believe they are going to pass in spite of the pressure.

The key is, you will perform as you see yourself performing in a classroom situation. If you have failed a previous test in this subject, forget it. If you believe you are going to fail the test, force the thought from your mind. The moment an experience or belief about yourself enters your mind and forms a picture, it becomes subjectively true. *Even if it is not.* So if you believe you are going to fail, even if you are well prepared, you probably will fail and almost certainly your grade will be lower than it could have been if you approached the matter by visualizing success.

Focus on success. Will yourself to remember the information you have heard in the classroom and apparently forgotten. Believe you are going to do well. Try it. What harm can it do?

Turn a Disadvantage to an Advantage

One young high school debater hated speaking in a hot auditorium. There was the sweat and the need for water and the smell of the perspiring audience. Generally the speakers and the listeners were uncomfortable and anxious for the program to end. Yet many high school auditoriums were hot and muggy. So, for a whole semester, she dreaded going into a competition on a hot day . . . and it affected her performance. She didn't win many debates.

But then she discovered imagery and some of the various techniques. She began to see not only herself, but everybody else, as uncomfortable. She realized that she wasn't the only one. And she saw that the heat was disturbing the performance of all of the speakers. Furthermore, she began to realize that if everybody was uncomfortable, she could use the heat to her advantage.

So she began to say to herself, "I can do this in spite of the heat."

"Everybody has to speak under the same conditions," she would repeat to herself, "but only I am aware that this is true.

"I can control my mind and body and overcome this heat.

"I can speak well in spite of the heat.

"I have a definite advantage over the others, since I am acknowledging the heat and my superiority over it.

"I can even take the audience's discomfort into consideration

"I have a real advantage.

"I have a real advantage.

"I have a real advantage."

Her inner perception of such situations became the key, and she began to win debates with regularity. She had learned how to use imagery, and confidence, to win instead of lose.

Build Up Your Visual Memory

There is a way to strengthen your "visual memory" to help on such occasions. By practicing this exercise, you will find that you will improve your ability to remember and recall thoughts, ideas and facts. Material you read in books will come back to you more easily, and so will facts and figures the teacher has written down for you.

The Reason for This Exercise
To help you improve your ability to recall data.

The Supplies You Will Need

Pen or pencil and ordinary bond paper.

How To Do The Exercise

• Divide the paper into twelve equal sections with pen or pencil lines. Ask a friend to fill in three or four of the squares in any random order, but to keep the paper covered. Uncover the paper for one second, then recover it. On another piece of paper, recreate the exact order of the blackened squares. Do this several times, with different patterns, until you can do it perfectly each time.

• Then increase the number of filled-in squares until you can do any six, any time, perfectly. This is an exercise you can do almost anywhere in spare time, if you have a friend around. It's fun.

• When this becomes child's play, substitute numbers for blackened squares. Your friend might put "3" in one square, "7" in another, and "9" in another. Soon you will be able to reproduce these patterns as well, but keep practicing with increasing difficulty, by increasing the number of numbers, all the way up to twelve.

The Result You May Expect

Before you know it, your visual memory will be improved. You'll be able to recall things you have seen without conscious effort. Your mind will be trained to remember. The more you practice this exercise, the better your visual memory will become, and soon schoolroom tests (or remembering the football playbook) will be much easier than before.

9

You Can Be a Sports Hero

Place kicker Frank Coral, who often kicked a field goal in the last few seconds to win a football game, was asked if he ever felt any pressure under those circumstances. "NO," he answered. "When I walked on the field I started visualizing the ball going through the uprights. It never occurred to me that I could miss."

Muscle Memory

Athletes know they have a "muscle memory" they can put to use through imagery. You can use this same trait to substantially improve your own performance on the court or field or rink or pool or course.

51

Here's a fact you may not know. You "blaze a trail" in your mind every time you do something, *anything*, be it success or failure. You have heard this in many ways. You have heard that a bad habit becomes worse and worse as you do it over and over again. You know that if you have a problem with your swing in baseball, you reinforce it each time you do it. It gets to be more of a problem with every swing. You are burning this swing into your muscle memory with each practice session. The more you do this, the tougher it is to change.

Every time you repeat an action, any action, the pattern becomes stronger and easier to follow again. These patterns are stored just like the tapes in a computer. This is true for any physical motion; athletics, dancing, gymnastics. If you do it right the first time, the action strengthens the second time, and the third time. If you do it *wrong* the first time, it also strengthens the second and third time.

But wrong actions can be changed through imagery. You can redirect your muscle memory into correct patterns. All you need do is learn how to recall the successful trails and reject the unsuccessful ones.

More about the science of this in the next chapter. Meanwhile, here's an exercise to help you begin to train your muscle memory.

The Reason for This Exercise

To gain complete familiarity with your playing area.

The Supplies You Will Need

The field, diamond, court, rink, or wherever you play and a friend. Also, a blindfold. For this explanation, let's use a basketball court, though you will be using your own game area.

How To Do The Exercise

• Walk onto the court and stand on a specific spot such as the foul line. Ask the friend to blindfold you. Then have him or her direct you to some other spot on the court.
"Move forward until you are directly under the basket."
"Back up to midcourt."
"Walk to the sideline."
"Walk to the corner."
"Walk back to the foul line."

The Result You May Expect

Each time you do this exercise, you will gain more and more familiarity with your area of play. You will be able to move with confidence in any direction, knowing exactly where you are even though you might be looking in any other direction.

More Muscle Memory Training

Here's another exercise to help you train your muscle memory for best possible performance on the sports field. Most athletes have, or can get, tapes or motion pictures of themselves in action. High schools generally tape games for players to study. But the problem is, the tapes show up all the mistakes the players are making as well as the good performances.

The Reason for This Exercise

To lock the movements of your very best performances into your muscle memory.

The Supplies You Will Need

Tapes or motion pictures of yourself in action and a full length mirror.

How To Do The Exercise

• See if it might be all right, through editing or copying, to take out the best parts of the tapes or films, the parts where you perform as perfectly as possible. This might be you hitting a home run perfectly, or spiking the ball (or dinking in) in volleyball, or executing the perfect layup in basketball. It could be you breaking out of the backfield and cutting back just right for a long run. It could be you leading a cheer, or marching perfectly in the band.

• These segments of tape or film should show you over and over again, as many times as possible in as many "perfect" situations as possible. Don't show your mistakes (we all make them), but only the times when you were performing at your best.

• Run this edited tape over and over and study it. Remember, in this case you are not interested in where you went wrong, as so many coaches tend to show, but in your skill. You want to see yourself at your best.

• Go over these performances in your mind again and again. Concentrate on how perfect each was and "look" at yourself doing each action in your mind. Repeat these actions before a full length mirror, concentrating on getting the motions just right, just as you recall from the film or tape.

• Do this as often as you can, as many times as you can.

The Result You May Expect

These visualizations, and repetitions, of you at your peak will be branded into your muscle memory. They will come back during game situations.

10

Exercise Your Brain as Well as Your Body

Mental exercises are imagery in its purest form. You are seeing yourself at your very best in your mind. It is even possible to see an entire game in this manner. You can see yourself at the beginning and how you are perfectly reacting to situations in the game. You can see yourself scoring, and winning the game.

Mental rehearsal such as this will help your game. You can even visualize the strategy you plan to use in the game. Are you going to be aggressive? Laid back? Cautious? Are you going to carry the game to this opponent, or allow them to carry it to you?

There is one caution where this mental rehearsal, this locking into the music memory, is concerned.

One golfer used imagery to help correct problems with his game. He saw himself in the difficult situations we all get into on the course. He would visualize (while commuting to and from work and at other "wasted" times) driving into the rough, or topping a ball, or missing an easy putt. He would visualize how he would handle these unhappy situations and attempt to turn them to an advantage. He would see himself driving from the rough and landing on the green, two feet from the cup, for example.

These techniques can help your game, but they should be practiced only well before the game. No later than a couple of days before the game, switch to positive images. Concentrate on confident, winning images, and not on problems you might have to face.

A Routine To Follow

1. See yourself getting up on game morning. You feel good. You feel like a winner.
2. See yourself dressing for the game. Everything looks just fine. Your uniform feels right, your equipment is ready.
3. See yourself entering the field or arena of play. You are calm and confident. You can feel that you are ready for the contest, ready to win.
4. As play progresses, see yourself just as you saw yourself in the films, making the right moves, executing the best plays, hitting the ball straight and true. Visualize the game going very well for your side.

5. Near the end of the game, see yourself ahead in the score and still playing well and without undue fatigue.
6. At last, see yourself leaving the arena a winner. Note how you are reacting to the cheers of the crowd and to your teammates if you have any.
7. Imagine yourself going over the winning game in your mind, once again fixing things into your muscle memory.

Do this mental exercise several times before each game. Try to feel as confident as possible, even if you are rated an underdog. Permit no negative thoughts to enter your mind.

Unrealistic? *Over*confidence? Not at all. It happens all the time that a team rated an underdog wins the game. Some athletes come on a field unwilling to lose. They simply will not acknowledge the possibility. It even happens that one confident athlete on a team inspires the rest of the team.

That athlete or competitor can (and should) be you.

11

Attack Your Weaknesses, And Know Why

At first, this matter of thinking your way to success might be a little difficult to swallow. All of us have lost. Even when we felt good about a game, we have lost. Even when we felt we were going to win, we lost.

And it is true that Martha, the young girl who wanted to be a running back on the high school football team, has little chance of success. She can probably think positively every waking moment and still not make the team. Note the word "probably," by the way, since imagery sometimes does amazing things. It could (and has) happened to people like Martha, But, generally speaking, Martha is going to find it very difficult to get on the team no matter what she does.

Cybernetics

Here's an interesting fact about cybernetics, the study of the brain and nervous system. Science has proved that the human brain and nervous system *cannot differentiate between a real and an imagined experience*. The body is absolutely controlled by the mind, yet the mind isn't sure of the difference between what is really happening, and what it thinks is happening. Or doesn't care. If you truly believe in your mind that your body is doing something (right or wrong, correctly or incorrectly) it will much more likely do it.

You limit your own potential by the mere fact of believing that you cannot do something well, or as well as somebody else. You must believe that you can do it better than anybody.

Your brain can help you to succeed, or fail, depending upon the information you feed it. Remember the experiment at the beginning of this book? The stone tossing experiment? Remember how you tossed the first half of the stones casually, then set the pattern into your brain that more of the stones will hit the tree? Much more often than not, you will hit the tree with greater regularity with the second half of the stones.

Such mental rehearsal is the key to better performances.

One engineer estimated that it would take a building many acres in size, jammed to the walls and filled to the ceiling with super-modern computers, to barely match the dullest human brain. The brain is a marvelous organ. Such a gigantic computer would still lack the power of your own brain.

It can store vast amounts of information and carry out programs just like a great computer, and it can do one other thing that a computer can't do. The brain can program itself. It can "think" in the truest sense, as well as self-correct. It can respond to changes around itself.

But this giant "machine" in your head can also hurt you. Not only do most of us not use this wonderful tool very well, but many doctors now suggest that there is a health concern we didn't even know we had. That is worry, itself. Remember the Harvard graduate study from Chapter Three?

Mental health, they are learning, plays a positive part in physical health. Can you think your way to cancer, or heart disease, or some other debilitating physical problem? Perhaps. It certainly seems true that if you think you are going to get sick, you have a greater chance of getting sick.

Through the brain, and imagery, good mental health offers a side benefit and that is better physical health.

How to Reduce Stress Through Thought

A young married girl became pregnant though neither she nor her husband felt they were ready for parenthood. What about college, for example? Terrible trouble, right? Not necessarily. She had dated the same boy since junior high. They were a couple. They were right for each other. Marriage had always been in their future and nobody, not even the parents of both, were more than normally upset.

It might not have been the best of situations, but they were married and in love. Both still planned to attend college, but now there would be a third person involved. All things considered, the problem could have been much more serious.

Except for one thing. She was terrified about having the baby. She was frightened and tense and full of apprehension. From the very first day she was so afraid that something would go wrong.

One of the two mothers suggested the "Lamaze" method of natural childbirth. Thus the pregnant girl, who had everything else going for her, learned one of the greatest secrets to reducing stress and tension. The key is the value of breath control to muscle relaxation. But what many prospective mothers, and athletes as well, don't realize is that a long, slow, deep breath is the body's way of telling the brain that it is back in control again.

Try it next time you are in a stressful situation. Take a deep breath. Hold it momentarily, then release it slowly. Tell your brain that everything is all right, that you are in control. Do it again if you wish. You are fighting the tendency to hold your breath, a message that tells the brain you are in trouble.

More Physical Ways to Contact the Brain

The idea behind all this cybernetics talk is to use your body to convince your brain to relax your body. Remember, the brain is in charge. What it says, goes. If it says everything is OK and that you are going to do well, you will do well. Stop and think. Identify why you are

tense. Are you angry, frightened, or anxious over an upcoming performance?

The situation may not change, but recognizing why
you feel as you do will make it easier to overcome your
tensions. Take some deep breaths while you do the following exercises to tell your brain that everything is
going to work out just fine.

1. Move your head slowly from side to side to release the tension in your neck muscles. Then
   move it back to front, slowly and easily. Then
   rotate your head, hanging it down and forward
   like a weight and rolling it slowly around to the
   side then back then side then front again. Reverse the direction and do it again.

   Perhaps somebody will massage your neck
   muscles. A cold cloth followed by a heating pad
   will also help to relax neck muscles, where tension often strikes first.

2. If you have been sitting too long, move your
   shoulders back and forth while you coil and un-
   coil your arms. Push them down, then draw them
   up. Get up and walk around if you can. Do some
   deep knee bends, then stretch your arms high
   over your head.

   If you have been standing too long, roll
   your knees back and forth to help take the pressure off your legs, thighs and stomach. Curl and
   uncurl your toes, then tighten and relax your
   thighs. Sit down if possible.

3. A quick and easy tension relaxer wherever you
   are is to tighten and then release all of the

muscles in your body. Do this to a count of eight; eight tight and eight relaxed, several times.

And *smile*! It is amazing how a smile relaxes the muscles of your face and decreases tension. Smile at yourself in a mirror if possible.

12

The Inner Peace Technique

Dr. Norman Vincent Peale developed positive thinking techniques that included relaxation methods. If you are tied up in knots over an impending matter, try this "inner peace" method for relaxing and telling your brain that you will survive.

1. Close your eyes, then empty your mind. Think of nothing at all. You can help by saying to yourself "I am now emptying my mind of irritation, worry, frustration and hate." Visualize them leaving.
2. Now say to yourself, "I am filling my mind with love, peace, calm and tranquility." Visualize each one as it enters your mind.

3. Take several deep breaths, letting each one out slowly. As you do so, allow your face muscles to completely relax.

4. Imagine peaceful scenes while you are repeating to yourself, "peace, tranquility, calm, serenity." Think "inner peace."

More Science

Bill was the star center on the school basketball team, but his life was being ruined by something outside of games and apparently out of his own control. Bill had a severe case of acne. His face was a mess, and it wasn't getting any better. He was a hero on the basketball court, but he had no social life at all. He tried everything, but nothing seemed to work. Bill was truly unhappy.

Science, of course, understands the physical causes of acne. Specific hormones increase to certain levels in the bloodstream and this produces changes in susceptible oil glands in the skin. There can be excessive production of oil, plugging of pores, stagnating, backing up and infection. Acne is the most common skin problem of all. Nine people out of ten suffer it to at least some extent. Medicines often don't help.

Science, however, moves on, and delves deeper into the mind. There is indirect evidence now that the *brain* can cause acne. It now appears possible that anxiety and nervous tension, problems Bill faces before and during every game in spite of his basketball talent, can aggravate acne through a neuro-endocrine mechanism coming from an area of the brain called the *hypothalamus*.

The hypothalamus, sensing Bill's tension, shoots off

a message to the pituitary, which relays the message on to the testes (or ovaries, in the case of a female) and the adrenals, the prime sources of the masculinizing hormones called androgens. If the androgens released into the bloodstream are not held there by binding proteins, they can escape into the tissues of the body and produce changes such as acne.

So it is possible that the tension and anxiety Bill feels because of his first love, basketball, might be causing his greatest problem, acne. It would not be wise to treat severe acne by treating the emotions alone, but it can't hurt.

Bill might continue his various medications and at the same time try some of the relaxation techniques here and as prescribed by his new doctor.

Still More Science

Marylou, a believer in the techniques of imagery, was a cheerleader and she took the job very seriously. Before a game, she would mentally rehearse the cheers, knowing that she would soon be performing before the entire student body and many parents and teachers. She didn't get too nervous or anxious because she used relaxation techniques to help prepare. She even exercised to help relax. As she did so, she began to experience a natural "high." She felt confident, and ready to go, and sure of herself. It was almost as though she had taken a calming drug. Of course, she hadn't, but there is a scientific basis for her feelings.

A healthy scientific basis.

Aerobic exercise can be one of the best methods

for relaxing, for relieving emotional and psychological stress. After about thirty minutes of relatively easy aerobic exercise, certain beta-endorphins and enkephalins are introduced into your system, and these natural morphinelike hormones help you to unwind and offer a feeling of well-being. They help you steady yourself and help you to use the natural skills you have practiced to do the best possible job. Marylou doesn't need anything artificial to help her prepare. She knows that exercise can help her feel better mentally, one of nature's natural and desirable secrets.

Marylou goes through another relaxing exercise you can use to prepare yourself. She becomes aware of her body and its tensions by lying down and relaxing. Then she closes her eyes and thinks of her toes. That's right, her toes. Then she "thinks" her way up her body. She asks herself, "Where do I feel tension and stress?" When she comes to a part of her body where these conditions exist, she focuses on loosening those muscles and making them relax.

Marylou is not unique. Watch winners as they prepare. You'll see them using these techniques before they "go on." Winners prepare differently than losers. Remember the 1984 L.A. Kings? They were often beaten as they skated onto the ice. Remember high jumper Dwight Stones? He prepared to win.

Winners Talk Differently Than Losers

Winners say "I can." Losers say "I'm not sure I can" or "I'll probably fail as I did once before" or "I wonder

if I can win today" or "Gee, I hope I can pass the test."
Winners take full responsibility for the actions in their
lives. They believe that life is a "do-it-yourself" program.

Certainly winners don't win every single time, nor
do losers lose every single time. But winners feel they
can win, even if, upon occasion, they may lose. And they
will win far more often than not, all other things being
at least reasonably equal. Losers, people who have no
real, deep-down confidence, sometimes win because of
the bounce of a ball or some other outside influence. But
generally, unless they are "lucky" in the matter of a
bouncing ball, they will lose.

Winners expect to pass the test while losers hope
they can pass it. This slight difference can be very important to you.

Make This Your Moment of Discovery

It is possible that you have been selling yourself short
all your life. Now you know that you can open up vast
new horizons. You are in the driver's seat. You can make
your own place in the world. You can accept the responsibility for your own health and happiness. If there are
those who would hold you back, or put down your efforts,
or "rain on your parade," ignore them and forge ahead
on your own "winners" path.

You know now that it isn't so much what happens
to you in life, but how you take it. Whether you allow
it to get you down.

You know that people are drawn to a confident,
optimistic, positive person. Such a person stands out as

plainly as the sweet smell of a barbeque on a warm summer evening, even if it is two blocks down the street. People are repelled by a negative, pessimistic person. People won't listen to a pessimist.

When they ask you why you always seem to feel so good and look so good and act so confidently, tell them you're on a new drug called "endorphin."

When they ask you if they can obtain some of it, tell them how.

13

You Must Learn to Concentrate

Jim and his date, Marcia, are enjoying a quick snack after the show. Nothing fancy, just a sandwich and coffee. Marcia has often kidded Jim about the fact that he laces his coffee with cream and sugar. She drinks hers black.

Sitting across from each other, they are enjoying a discussion of the show they have just seen. Then the coffee is served.

"I guess you want some 'weakeners' to add . . . ?" she jokes.

"I guess so," Jim drawls back. Both enjoy the difference in taste, and neither minds the banter.

Then, from the end of the table, the cream and sugar containers slide over to Jim.

Wait a minute! They *slide* over to Jim? Pushed by Marcia, right?

Wrong.

So Jim spills his coffee from shaking hands and Marcia screams and faints, right?

Wrong, again.

The pleasant conversation continues while Jim adds the correct portions of each to his steaming coffee.

Yes, there is a trick here. Not in the restaurant table, but in the fact that this scene takes place far in the future. Jim, needing the cream and sugar, merely *wills* it to come across the table. Marcia could do the same. That's why she isn't at all disturbed by what happened.

In fact, when their snack is finished they are planning to "transport" themselves in the best "beam me up, Scotty" tradition to Jim's weekend place on the moon.

Experts in the mind know that we use only a minor portion of our brain. Many feel that eventually we will use most of it, and the power Jim exhibited might be routine.

All of this is imagery of the future. Imagery of today is just beginning, but it can be a great help to you. Not if you do it only once. For any real value, imagery must be constant and repeated over a period of time. Nor should you expect to be able to concentrate to best advantage at first. The important thing is to be regular and consistent. If your mind wanders, if distractions occur, let them come and then gently bring your mind back to the image being worked on.

Controlling Your Attention

If you have ever had a chance to go to a professional golf competition, you know that it is necessary for the "gallery" to be silent when the pro is teeing off or putting. The errant flight of an airplane can completely upset a pro golfer's shot, and they react with a glare.

Yet a football player can execute the most complicated play with thousands of people screaming at the top of their lungs. And a basketball player can sink a foul shot with hundreds of people waving hands and shouting to distract him or her.

It is all a matter of concentration, and what we are accustomed to hearing. Most pro golfers could play just as well, but they have become used to quiet and so they have come to depend upon it.

John, a senior in high school and a star on the baseball team, used to have a real problem in concentrating. Opposing catchers had a "book" on John. They knew about him and would stir about and even comment under their breath in an effort to rattle him as he stood at the plate. More times than not, it would work, and John's batting average remained dangerously low.

Then, using the following technique, which you can adjust to your own activity, John learned to concentrate on the job at hand. It wasn't long before his batting average climbed. He learned to prevent distractions through imagery.

Learning to Concentrate

1. At first, in his own bedroom, John practiced gaining and holding a mental image of himself at the plate. That's all, just standing at the plate ready to hit. If he found his attention wandering, he would say "Concentrate" quietly to himself, then he would regain the mental picture.

2. John began to keep track of his times of concentration. He would punch a stopwatch as he began to concentrate, then punch it again the moment his attention drifted. He would log these times. He noted a definite increase in the times as he practiced.

3. John began to be secure in his concentration, so he moved his practice from the quiet of his room to places where there was more noise. He tried it while watching TV with his family, or at the beach, or at school. Again he timed himself, and again his times improved.

4. Finally, John told his friends and teammates what he was doing. He asked for their help. He asked them to attempt to distract him. He asked them to comment on his form at the plate, or even on what he was wearing or how he had combed his hair. He wanted them to pick at him personally while he was attempting to concentrate on his image of himself at the plate. It wasn't long before John was able to concentrate for the time it would take him to step up to the plate and get a hit.

Try it. It *works*. Before long you will be able to give full attention to the task at hand, even though you might have been distracted by what is going on around you.

At this point, you can begin to practice mental imagery on your form and style. You can begin to see yourself doing the job perfectly. You will be using the same technique used by Russian athletes as they sit in the stands and watch the others sweating.

You will be able to use imagery to help you in many areas of your life. Imagery can help you handle grief, meet people, or make a speech. It can even help you in weight and posture control, in general health and happiness.

14

Using Imagery in Your Daily Life

Imagery can be used in many ways in your everyday life. Here are some of them.

Like To Quit Smoking?

First, decide *why* . . . then *do it*! Cold turkey, with no looking back. Easier than it sounds? Perhaps, but read on. You have learned of the power of your own mind. Now *use* it!

There are three rules to follow.

> 1. List the reasons why you smoke. These could include habit, a way of finishing a meal, a way

of starting the day, a fear of seeming unsociable in a smoking group, or merely not wanting to be pushed into something because of negative advertising or peer pressure. Or it could include the pure enjoyment of smoking.

2. List the reasons why you would like to quit smoking. These could include a concern for your health, the cost of smoking, the fact that smoking is no longer a part of modern society's lifestyle, the fact that a loved one doesn't smoke, or the fact that smoking is nothing more than an undesirable habit bringing little to your life.

3. Plan to keep physically and mentally busy with things that really interest you during your withdrawal.

Then . . . *QUIT*!

Say to yourself, "I won't smoke again, ever! Smoking is over, finished, done, out!" Imagine yourself as a nonsmoker in every situation. Hear yourself in your imagination saying, "No, thanks," when somebody offers you a cigarette, then say it.

You are giving no reason and having no doubts. Make the announcement to your body when you are relaxed, feeling good, and mentally strong and alert. Allow your brain to do its job. Your body doesn't want to smoke, so give your powerful brain the job of seeing that it desn't. Don't look back. Don't even consider looking back.

When times get a little tough, say to yourself, "I care for my body. I love myself," as often as you need.

When you simply must have a smoke, say to yourself "I can wait a few more minutes" then "I can wait another hour" then "I can wait another day for the sake of my beautiful body."

Believe in what you are doing. Believe that imagery will work for you.

Are You Grieving?

Have you ever lost somebody or something you really loved? It is a devastating experience. Most of us eventually get over the loss, though it is very difficult, but some grieve for years.

June was a good example of this. She lost her father when she was nine. At sixteen she was still grieving. Her mother couldn't help her, nor could her friends. She would apparently be having a good time, then suddenly she would remember her father and begin weeping. June had never been able to resolve the loss in her mind.

Finally, June began to use imagery to help her reconcile the death of her father.

Dr. Frederick Towne Melges, professor of psychiatry at Duke University, listed some of the signs of unresolved grief.

1. Continued yearning for the loved one. Often the deceased is referred to as in the present. Dreams of a reunion are not uncommon. Pictures and mementos are kept and touched as though an eventual reunion is possible.

2. The survivor feels that the deceased must be "kept alive" in the heart so that unspoken expressions of love might still be possible.

3. Possible anger at the deceased is misdirected to one's self. This is a result of the anger the survivor feels for the deceased "leaving" and is often followed by guilt for being angry in the first place.

4. Fear that the deceased, now "all knowing" in the spiritual world, has become aware of secrets kept from them while living.

5. The bereaved makes a silent vow to remain faithful, a contract that promises to remain with the deceased, to stay by their side forever.

6. Some bereaved receive a secondary gain from their sadness. They realize that others will continue to emotionally support them as long as they are grief-stricken. Or, if the support from others is short-lived, they cling to the memory of the support they once had from their loved one now gone.

June faced all of these to some degree, until she used imagery. With imagery, she was able to "give up" her father and cure her depression.

Dr. Melges technique involves recalling the affection between the living and the deceased—painful but it reestablishes the self-identity and worth of the bereaved. Then the bereaved visualizes the death and funeral and burial as though it were happening in the present. June even engaged in a dialogue with her father in which she discussed her fears, her anger, her secrets, and the other matters that had been bothering her.

Finally, sadly, June said goodbye to her father, and heard him bid her farewell (though at first she could only say "goodbye for now"). Imagery allowed June to see her father in the present and not in the past, and helped her overcome her grief.

Using Imagery to Control Weight

"Porky" was embarrassed about his weight. For years he had been overweight, and the others at school had long since given up on him. So much so, in fact, that they used his nickname not to be cruel, but merely because he was fat. Porky was miserable. He had gone through diet after diet and many weight-loss programs without success. The problem was, he simply loved to eat.

Inside his fat body was a lean, healthy body wanting to get out, but Porky just didn't have the "will power" to lose weight.

Then he learned a great secret. He learned about imagery. He was able to "see" himself slim for the first time. Here's how he did it.

The Paper Bag Technique

Don't laugh at poor Porky for the way he started his new regime. He went to his bedroom, took off his clothes, put a paper bag over his head (with eyeholes cut into it), then studied himself before a full length mirror. He looked at a front view, a side view and a rear view of this "stranger" before him in the mirror. By covering his face, Porky was able to disassociate himself from the image.

What he saw was ridiculous. This was somebody he felt needed to lose weight—and fast. Porky looked until he was convinced that this person was in serious trouble.

Then Porky used the old "doctor's examining room" gambit.

Go See a Doctor . . . In Your Mind

1. Porky visualized himself naked in a doctor's examining room. There was the paper-covered examining table, the cabinet of supplies, and the scales. You know the kind. Porky could visualize it very clearly. You stand on the scale's floor platform, then move weights back and forth on the balance bar. Porky had been on them before.

2. In his imagination, he stepped on the scales. He moved the weights and read his weight. It was far too much, and Porky knew it. But he was in his room, alone, visualizing, so nobody else could see it.

3. Then Porky had some serious fun. He stepped off the scale, in his imagination, then stepped back on. This time he moved the scales to his desired weight and the bar balanced perfectly. He weighed exactly what he hoped to weigh. He felt wonderful in this visualization. He knew how good it felt to have reached this very difficult goal. He reveled in the feeling.

4. This very powerful visualization allowed him (or *you*) to realize vividly how good it feels to be slim and trim as well as understand the detrimental effects of overeating. Porky was able to "see" himself at his desired weight, and this is strong motivation.

5. He went through this mental exercise again and again, each time reinforcing the positive feeling of being at his desired weight. He found that he was gradually able to resist food he would normally have gobbled up without thinking. He found that each time such food was offered, the image of himself naked in the examining room at his full-blown weight *interfered*. This was quickly followed by the pleasant feeling of seeing himself on scales showing his desired weight. The fact that he had achieved this goal, even in his imagination, was powerful help.

It worked for Porky, and it will work for you.

Overeating, according to many experts, is often stress-related. This might not even be something you recognize, since some of this stress can come from deep within you, from one of the most deep-seated anxieties in all humans, the fear of being hungry. Porky learned to enjoy, truly enjoy, the food he permitted himself. He learned to *believe* that he would be satisfied physically and mentally with those portions.

Another technique is the "closed door" system. Once you have fixed the examining room scales firmly in your mind, try this.

The Closed Door System

1. In your imagination you are walking down a crowded street with people all around. You don't know any of them, but they are pushing and shoving each other and you. You want to get to your destination, a safe and secure refuge. Suddenly you come upon a closed door.

2. You know that behind the door is the obstacle that is preventing you from eating sensibly, from permanently losing weight. So you open the door, look at the obstacle (weakness, anger, stress, lack of will power, or whatever else is preventing you from losing weight), say to yourself *"This will no longer prevent me from reaching my slim and trim goal!"*

3. Then you slam the door and walk quickly away from the pushing crowds to your safe haven. Relax there until you are again calm and peaceful.

It is difficult at first to believe, but this mind-journey, which allows you to slam the door, to close out the thing that is preventing you from losing weight, is powerful. You can do it again and again. It will help you to uncover some of the barriers holding you back. There may be different barriers on each trip. You might be surprised at what you find behind the door, but you'll slam the door and mentally remove the barrier anyhow. The more problems you face and dismiss, the better your chances of slimming down.

This sort of imagery training will bring about new

eating patterns. The obstacles might be different for each "fatty," many of whom have gone through diet after diet with little or no permanent success, but it will work for everybody.

The mind can be the most powerful tool of all to help you lose weight. All you have to do is *use* it.

15

Imagery ... And One of the Worst Fears of All

Perhaps you have felt it. Most of us have. It is that cold, clammy, half-sick feeling you get as you come closer and closer to a public speech. Feel it? Rodney usually got nervous, but forged ahead. Richard became sick to his stomach with "butterflies" before he went on. Marion remained physically ill through half of her speech until finally she would get involved in what she was doing and forget her fear.

Suzanne actually fainted before one of her performances in front of a crowd.

None of them used imagery to help.

Warren did, though at one time he was just as terrorized as any of the others. But Warren learned that public speaking can become a breeze through the power of the mind. Warren, who was once filled with fear and a nervous physical wreck at the thought of delivering a speech to his class, came to love the idea of getting up to perform.

Warren used two techniques to help himself.

The First Technique

Warren understood what all the others had learned, that a talk must have (a) a central idea, (b) that the speaker must know the audience, and (c) that the talk should have a beginning, a middle and an end.

Simple enough, but very important. These are basics. You've probably heard speakers who ramble on with "I've been asked to speak on . . ." or "The point I would like to make is . . ." or "Before I begin, I'd like to say . . ." or even "Unaccustomed as I am to public speaking . . ."

A speech must be organized, with notes on the key points and a note or two of transition from one point to the next. Warren learned that memorizing a speech is wrong. He knew that if he committed a speech to memory, then forgot a line, he would "dry up."

Warren realized that he should step to the podium and give his talk. But even though he knew these things, he was still terrified about the actual presentation. Would they listen? Would they laugh at him? Would he make a fool of himself? Would he get a terrible grade, or no applause at all?

These thoughts plagued Warren.

The Second Technique

Then Warren began to use imagery. He fixed into his mind the fact that what he had to say was something the audience wanted to hear, otherwise why had he been asked to speak in the first place? He was the expert. Even in a classroom situation, and certainly in a full-blown public speech, Warren held the thought that he had researched and prepared, that he knew the facts, that he had anecdotes that would interest and amuse his audience.

He even began to see his audience as children who were waiting with anticipation to hear his words. In fact, this is generally true. Most audiences are there to hear. They have no idea what you are going to say, so if you make a mistake they don't even know it. They are not there, in most cases, to judge or condemn or even rate the speaker. They are there to hear what the speaker has to say.

It amused Warren to picture his audience in their nightclothes. This, in fact, helped him to maintain eye contact, to look about his audience with authority and inner calm. After all, he was the only one fully dressed.

Most important, a week before his speech, Warren began to prepare the presentation. Every day, in otherwise wasted time, Warren would see himself in his imagination walking to the podium, or before the class. He is calm and perfectly confident. His speech is ready and he is even anxious to deliver it. In his imagination, Warren can see the positive reaction to his opening comments. If it is an amusing anecdote, he can hear the laughter. If it is a serious or hard-hitting opening, he can hear the gasps. He is in control.

Then, as his speech progresses, he can see in his imagination that it is going far better than he had ever dared hope. The audience is obviously enjoying, for they seem to lean closer so they won't miss a word. There is no disturbance in the room, no whispering or other signs of lack of interest. He can see that his talk is hitting home. He can see that his facts are holding them.

As he nears the conclusion of his imaginary talk, he can see that he is really enjoying himself. This speech is working. He'd like to try it again, before a larger audience. In fact, he wishes the room was larger, so that more people could hear.

In his mind, Warren concludes his speech with a confident summing up and the audience can do nothing but cheer. And they do. The speech, once so frightening, has become one of the most pleasant experiences in Warren's life.

This imagery approach will work if you give it a chance. It'll work in public speaking, and it'll work in most other areas of your life. It's fun, and it won't cost a cent.

Here are two final exercises to practice.

The Reason for This Exercise

To help improve your visual memory and general visualization skills and to help enhance your sense of visual space.

The Supplies You Will Need

Pencil and sheets of paper

How To Do The Exercise

• Draw a diagram of your homeroom at school. Include the teacher's desk, bookcases, arrangement of chairs, all the details you can recall. Do this in less than two minutes, then check it against the real room later.

• Draw a diagram of your room at home, including location of bed, dresser, doors, and all the other details you can recall. Do this in less than two minutes, then check it against the real room later.

• Draw a diagram of your school, including rooms, offices, auditorium, gymnasium, and all the other details you can recall. Do this in less than two minutes, then check it against the real school later.

• Draw a diagram of your home (this is not easy), including the rooms, garage, and all the other details you can recall. Do this in less than two minutes, then check it later.

The Result You May Expect

First, don't be discouraged if you miss many details. This is not an easy exercise. But this exercise will improve your visual memory and enhance your visualization skills. Do the exercise again and again using different locations until you can do them as nearly perfectly as possible.

_____

And one fun exercise to practice with.

_____

The Reason for This Exercise

To continue to improve your general imagery skills.

The Supplies You Will Need
A deck of cards.

How To Do The Exercise

• Deal out a hand of poker, bridge, or any other favorite card game. Play it out. Then recall the hand and try in your mind to play out all the possible options. What if you had dealt yourself an ace instead of a king? A spade instead of a heart? How would this have affected the play? What if you had been playing bridge instead of poker, or poker instead of bridge. Examine these options in your mind, and attempt to play out the resulting hands. Do this for fun, in relaxing time.

The Result You May Expect

This type of practice will continue to improve your visual skills and enhance your ability to imagine results other than what actually happened.

Enjoy imagery. It's fun, and it can improve your life in many ways. You'll know this is true if you give imagery a chance.

Bibliography

Adams, James L. *Conceptual Blockbusting*, Scribners.

Bunker, Linda J. & Rotella, Robert J. *Mind, Set and Match*, Spectrum.

Kosslyn, Stephen M. *Ghosts in the Mind's Machine*, W.W. Norton.

Peale, Norman Vincent. *Positive Imaging*, Revell.

Sherman, Harold. *Your Power to Heal*, Harper & Row.

Waitley, Dr. Denis. *The Winner's Edge*, Berkley.

Index

acne, 66-67
ACTH, 43
aerobic' exercise, 67-68
alpha state, 24

basketball, 7
Blumberg, Judy, 5
brain paths, 21-22
brain exercise, 56-58
Bry, Adelaide, 19-20
Burns, Dr. David D., 32, 34
Burr, Harold, 19

Cambridge University, 23
Cerf, Bennett, 19

choke sign, 42, 44
Cognitive Therapy, 32
Colorado State University, 17
concentration, 71-75
confidence, 28-34
confidence tape, 35-38
Coral, Frank, 51
Cousins, Norman, 18-19
cybernetics, 60-64

daydreaming, 10-11, 15-20,
   23-26
Dionne, Marcel, 31

Eastman, Max, 19

Enjoyment of Laughter, The, 19
Esalen Sports Institute, 11

Feeling Good: The New Mood Therapy, 32
Funt, Allan, 19

Garfield, Dr. Charles, 22
Geller, Uri, 23
Go See the Movie in Your Head, 20
Goldenson, Robert, 26
grieving, 78-79

Harvard, 18
Hill, Professor Harold, 3-4
hypothalamus, 66-67

I.Q., 10
inner peace, 65

Jacobson, Edmund, 20
Jenner, Bruce, 30, 35

Kings, Los Angeles, 31, 35, 68

Lamaze, 62
Lopez, Nancy, 27
luck, 8-9

Marx Brothers, 19
McDonnell Foundation, 23
McDonnell Laboratory, 23
Melges, Dr. Frederick Towne, 78-79
Michelangelo, 24
muscle memory, 51-55
Music Man, The, 3

Nash, Ogden, 19
New England Journal of Medicine, 17
Nicklaus, Jack, 45-46

Peale, Norman Vincent, 65
Pennsylvania State University, 10
Perelman, S. J., 19
Phillips, Peter R., 23
public speaking, 85-88

Reinhardt, Alexandra, 27
reverse imagery, 9

Sea Pines Resort, 11
Seibert, Michael, 4
Selye, Dr. Hans, 18
Shorr, Joseph E., 20
Simmer, Charlie, 31
smoking, 76-77
South Carolina, 11
Spano, Mike, 11
speaking, public, 85-88
spoon benders, 22-23
Stanford University, 23
Stanley Cup, 31
Stones, Dwight, 46, 68
Subtreasury of American Humor, 19
Suinn, Richard, 17

Taylor, Dave, 31
tension, 39-42
Think System, 4
Thurber, James, 19
Trevino, Lee, 28
trial and error, 16
Triple Crown Line, 31

visualization, 11-14, 17-18
*Visualization: Directing the
    Movies of Your Mind*, 19
visual memory, 49-50

Wagman, Morton, 24
wart healers, 22-23

Washington University, 23
weight control, 80-84
White, E. B. & Katherine, 19
Willson, Meredith, 3-4
Wodehouse, P. G., 19

Yale School of Medicine, 19